DIOR

CHRISTIAN
DIOR

For Janice Hess,
my mother.

Just like Dior,
your enormous heart
has led you through life.

CHRISTIAN DIOR

THE ILLUSTRATED WORLD OF A FASHION MASTER

Megan Hess

Hardie Grant

BOOKS

CONTENTS

INTRODUCTION

The name Christian Dior is synonymous with fashion. The man who spawned the New Look, the classic Bar Suit and the Miss Dior fragrance revolutionised the way women dressed in the 1940s and 50s, becoming one of France's most famous sons in the process.

A RELATIVELY LATE BLOOMER, DIOR burst onto the fashion scene in 1947 aged forty-two, but he quickly became one of the most influential couturiers the world has ever seen. He conceived of silhouettes that paired creative vision with technical precision and his designs were the height of feminine opulence.

As a designer, Dior sold a dream of complete extravagance and beauty, but in fact he was no stranger to poverty and pain.

Born into a wealthy family during a golden era for France, Dior led a remarkable life punctuated with ups and downs – from the Great Depression and two world wars, to family tragedy and illness. Through his experiences of hardship and austerity, Dior never lost sight of the importance of creativity and elegance.

A private man who stood reluctantly in the spotlight and was intensely superstitious, Dior was also an astute businessman. He took his designs from a small workshop in the heart of Paris and created a vast enterprise with an international audience within the space of just a decade.

Even today his legacy is almost unrivalled. The Christian Dior spirit has endured for over seventy years under the guidance of the six incredible designers who have succeeded him. Each of them has left their own mark on the brand and ensured the name Dior remains at the very heart of style.

It is time to discover a truly extraordinary man who lived through one of the most tumultuous times in history and changed the course of fashion forever.

THE
MAN

CHRISTIAN DIOR THE COUTURIER was a creative sensation, the head of a global company and one of the most celebrated designers of the twentieth century. But Christian Dior the man was much more reserved and private than his public persona would suggest.

Born into a wealthy family during a period of prosperity in France and living through huge upheaval in his younger years, he spent most of his life in relative anonymity.

Though it was written in destiny that he would become a huge success, Dior didn't make his mark in the world of couture until he was forty-two. It took a lifetime of experience and some remarkable friendships before Christian Dior would become the couturier we know today.

Christian Dior was born on
21 January 1905 in Granville,
Normandy, the second of five
children in a well-off family.

His mother and father, Madeleine and
Maurice, owned a successful fertilizer
business that provided them and their
children, Raymond, Christian, Jacqueline,
Bernard and Catherine, a comfortable life.

The Dior family home was Les Rhumbs, a grand villa perched on top of cliffs facing out across the sea to the Channel Islands. The house, with its classic Anglo-Norman styling and colour palette of soft rose pink and grey, would be hugely influential to Christian over the years.

Young Christian was a dreamer. He spent
an idyllic childhood in Granville under the
loving eye of Madeleine, an avid gardener
who transformed the windswept grounds
of Les Rhumbs into an English-style garden
filled with roses and lilies of the valley.

Christian adored his elegant mother
and embraced her love of flowers.

He could often be found working
alongside her in the garden.

"

AFTER WOMEN, flowers are the LOVELIEST THING God has given THE WORLD.

"

Christian would also spend hours in his own
world, reading books or learning the names
of flowers from horticultural catalogues,
or sitting in the warmth of the linen room
in the company of the women who would
sing as they worked.

To him, these were the happiest
times of his childhood.

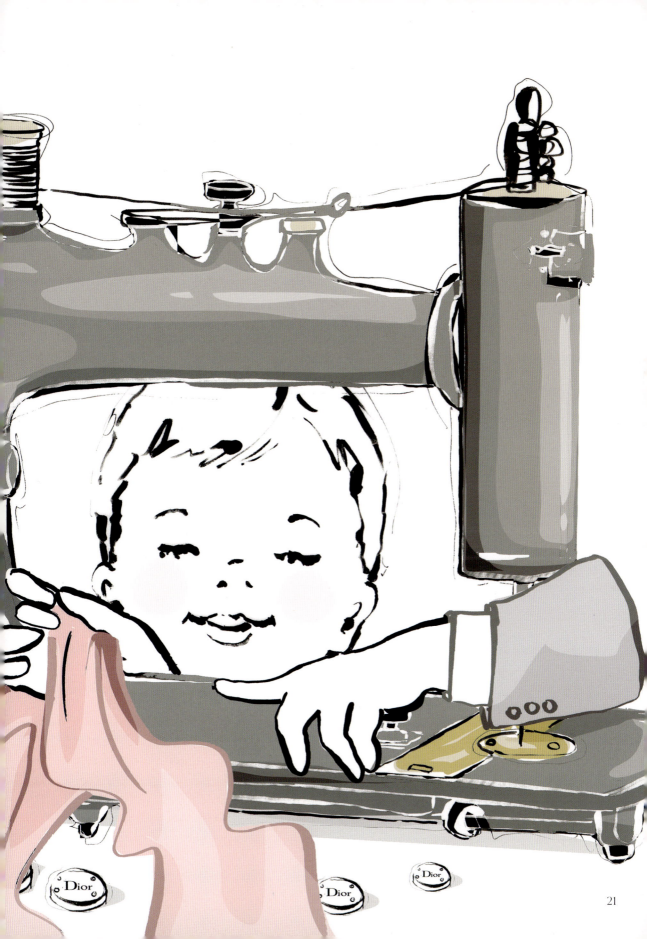

When Christian was five, the Dior family moved to an apartment in the 16th arrondissement of Paris.

It was 1910 and the final days of the Belle Époque.

This flourishing period of creativity left a mark on the young boy as he absorbed the energy of a city bursting with optimism, elegance and progress.

In 1914, these happy times would
come to an abrupt end with the
arrival of World War I.

As the gloom of war descended
over Paris, the Dior family was
holidaying back at Granville.

They would remain at Les Rhumbs
for the duration of the conflict,
finding a safe haven in the tranquil,
protected paradise.

It was during this time Dior had his first encounter with a clairvoyant. He was working at a charity fair for soldiers in Granville when a palm reader offered to tell his fortune.

She gave an incredible prediction: 'You will be penniless, but women will be good to you and it is thanks to them that you will succeed. You will make large profits and be obliged to make numerous crossings.'

The Dior family was still in possession of a sizable fortune and, despite the war, had little inkling of the tough financial times around the corner. The teenaged Christian, moreover, wasn't known for his adventurous spirit. There was little chance he'd be travelling across the globe.

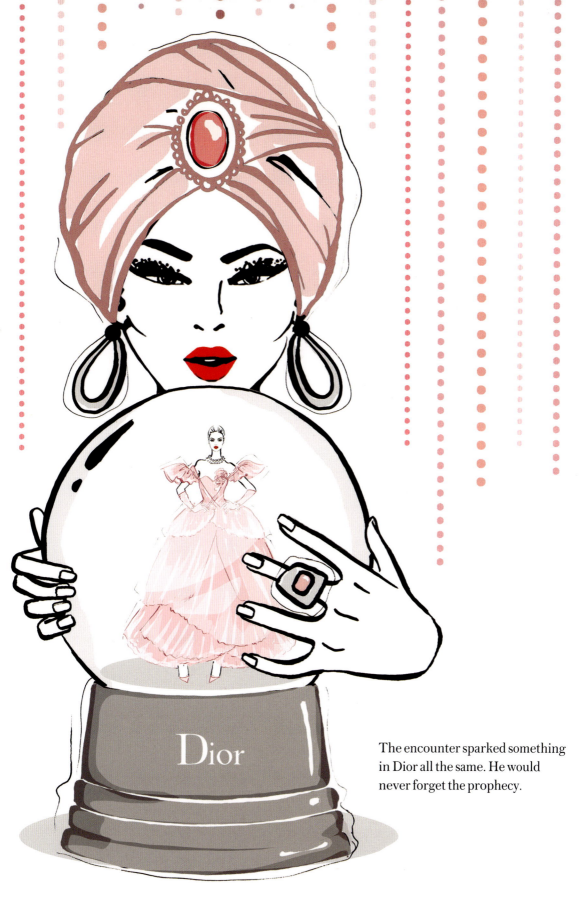

The encounter sparked something
in Dior all the same. He would
never forget the prophecy.

When the war was over, the Dior family moved
back to Paris and Christian dreamt of pursuing a
career in architecture. Instead, he was pressured
by his family to study political science.

Madeleine and Maurice Dior were keen
for their second son to be a diplomat and
wouldn't support his more creative pursuits.

Dior enrolled at the Paris Institute of Political
Studies but dropped out shortly after, far more
interested in music, literature, painting and
the new friendships he was forming in the city,
which was once again alive with bohemian spirit.

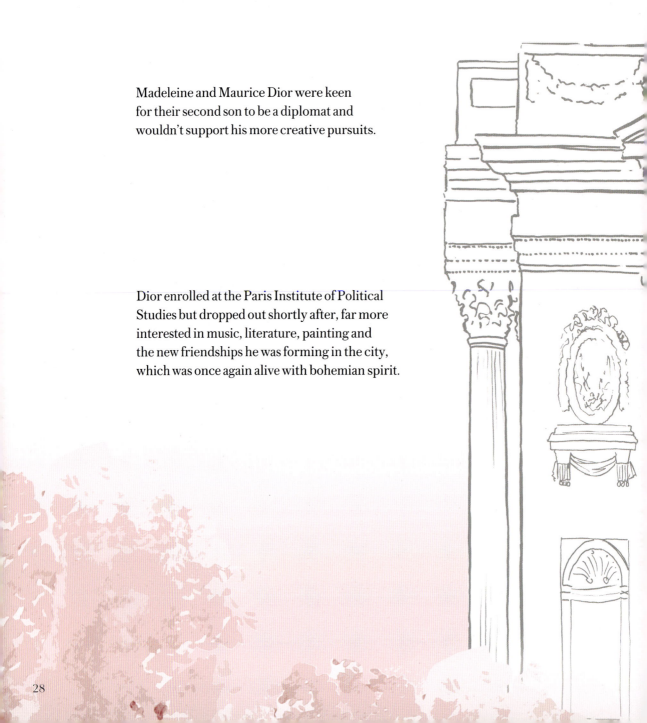

École Libre des Sciences Politiques

> "

Paris,
ALIVE WITH
inventions,
COSMOPOLITAN,

intelligent,
PRODIGAL WITH
truly novel
NOVELTIES.

"

In 1928 he opened an art gallery with friend Jacques Bonjean.

Finally succumbing to the idea that their son was drawn to the arts, Madeleine and Maurice Dior gave the venture their blessing and backed it financially.

They gave Christian just one condition: the Dior family name was not to appear above the gallery door. No son of theirs was to be seen as a 'lowly shopkeeper'.

35

It was an incredible time to be involved in the art scene in Paris.

The surrealist movement was gaining force and Dior's little gallery on Rue La Boétie showed an almost unbelievable roster of high-profile artists.

It was also, however, a tough time to be making a living. When the Great Depression arrived, Gallery Jacques Bonjean was forced to shut its doors.

Undeterred, Dior joined another friend, Pierre Colle, to open a second gallery in 1932, on Rue Cambacérès.

Here, he showed artists such as Georges Braque, Pablo Picasso, Jean Cocteau and Max Jacob.

Galerie d'art

Fermé

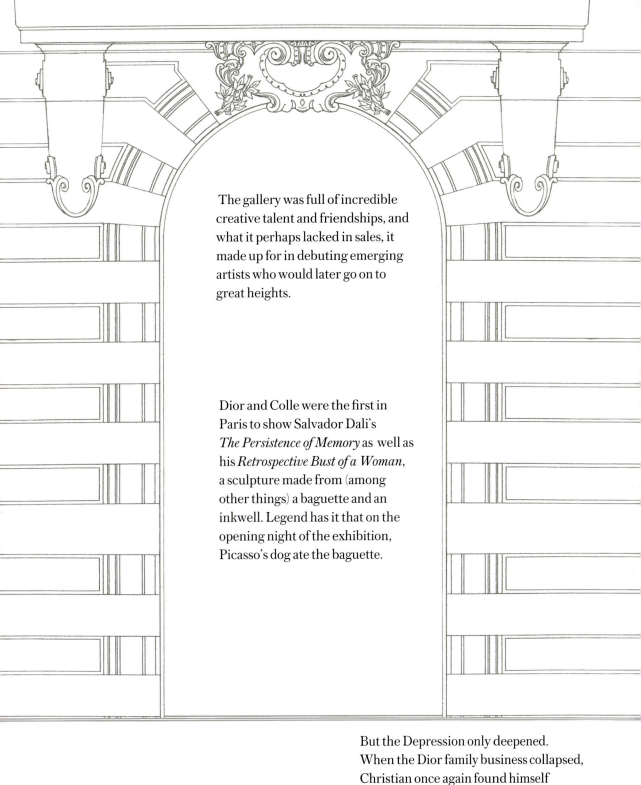

The gallery was full of incredible creative talent and friendships, and what it perhaps lacked in sales, it made up for in debuting emerging artists who would later go on to great heights.

Dior and Colle were the first in Paris to show Salvador Dali's *The Persistence of Memory* as well as his *Retrospective Bust of a Woman*, a sculpture made from (among other things) a baguette and an inkwell. Legend has it that on the opening night of the exhibition, Picasso's dog ate the baguette.

But the Depression only deepened. When the Dior family business collapsed, Christian once again found himself shuttering the doors of the gallery.

Dior's career as a gallerist was over,
his family fortune had dried up, and the
tough times were about to get worse.

Within a year, his beloved mother would die
and one of his brothers, Bernard, would be
interned in a psychiatric institution.

Dior spent the next few years impoverished, sometimes sleeping on a friend's floor or sharing an attic.

He had to sell the last of the paintings from his galleries in order to support his family.

He maintained times were still happy, writing that he and his friends would 'keep away the mice as we invented fantastic amusements' with the help of a piano, a gramophone or fancy dress games.

But the harsh living arrangements took their toll. Dior contracted tuberculosis and left Paris to spend a year recovering in the mountains.

It was during this convalescence that he was truly able to discover his own creativity, teaching himself to draw and returning again and again to sketching fashion.

He began selling his sketches to newspapers, fashion houses and milliners, and realised he could make a living as a fashion illustrator.

His work eventually caught the eye of Swiss
couturier Robert Piguet, who offered Dior a job
as a pattern maker in his Paris couture house.

Dior loved Paris and immersing himself in the world of fashion.

He once walked past a small townhouse on Avenue Montaigne and remarked that he would one day open a couture house at the address.

But Dior's first real break into the world of haute couture would soon be cut short by the forces of history.

In 1939 dark clouds were once again forming over France. World War II broke out, and people began tightening their belts, giving up all extravagances in support of the war efforts.

Dior was called away from his job at Piguet to serve in the military, although he luckily avoided active duty, instead working on a farm.

In June 1940, the French government capitulated to the Nazi regime and many of the couture houses in Paris shut their doors – some of them for good.

Dior's youngest sister, Catherine, had a
very different experience of the war. She
joined the French Resistance, couriering
documents at great personal risk.

Tragedy struck when she was arrested
by the Nazis in 1944 and sent to a
concentration camp. Distraught at the
idea that he would never see his sister
alive again, Dior consulted his fortune
teller, who urged him not to worry.

It wasn't until 1945, nine months after
Catherine had been captured and long after
Paris had been liberated, that the fortune
teller's prediction would come true.

Dior received a phone call telling him
that his sister would be arriving in the
city by train the following day.

When Catherine stepped onto the
platform she was severely emaciated,
in poor health and clearly suffering from
the effects of trauma, but she was alive.

She would go on to be
recognised as a war hero
and awarded many honours.

55

Dior was aghast at the fashions
that emerged during the war.

Around the world governments had brought in austerity measures forbidding any embellishments in women's clothes.

Strict controls on materials of all kinds were imposed, the number of pockets allowed on a garment were limited, and pleats, frills and bows disappeared.

Dior hated the effect austerity had on the way women dressed and was saddened by what seemed to be the death of the French couture industry.

But as the world emerged from the war years, the spectre of poverty and misery gave way to hope. And Dior found himself working as a pattern maker at Lucien Lelong, the largest and most prestigious couture house in Paris.

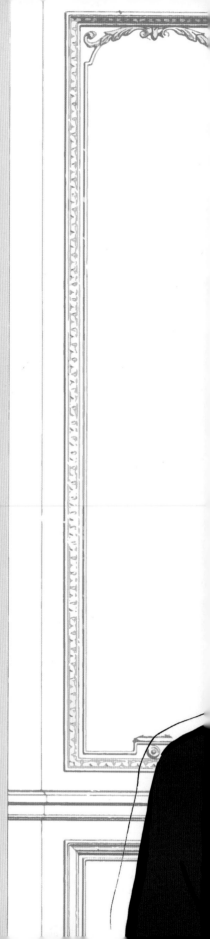

LUCIEN LELONG

Carmel Snow

He started making friends among
the fashion crowd, including
the legendary editor-in-chief of
Harper's Bazaar, Carmel Snow.

Dior was happy at Lelong,
learning the tradition of
fine craftsmanship and
working alongside
Pierre Balmain, who
would also go on to become
a master of couture.

But a chance meeting in 1946 with a childhood friend would set Dior on an unexpected new path.

"
Chance always COMES TO THE AID of those who REALLY WANT HER.

"

Dior's friend Georges Vigouroux told him about the wealthy businessman Marcel Boussac, who was looking for someone to take over a flagging couture house in his group.

Dior told his friend he knew of no-one suitable. It took two more discussions with Vigouroux before the humble designer thought to put himself forward for the opportunity.

During an early meeting with Boussac, however, Dior entirely surprised himself by boldly refusing the offer of the top job and instead asking the wealthy businessman to back a new couture house – in Dior's own name.

The sudden bout of confidence paid off and Boussac agreed immediately, but Dior was again full of uncertainty. He consulted his fortune teller, who urged him to accept the offer.

Still mulling over the decision, Dior was walking down Rue du Faubourg Saint-Honoré when he hit his foot on a small metal star.

It was most likely a piece that had fallen from the wheel of a cart, but to the designer it was Fate herself calling out to him, giving him an evening star to guide him to his destiny.

Christian Dior

He pocketed the star, and with
that his mind was made up.

The House of Dior was born.

THE
BRAND

ONCE THE DECISION WAS MADE to launch Maison Dior, the reluctant designer felt immense responsibility to make it a success. He pushed aside all personal doubt and at once took on a new public persona – that of the worldly couturier and savvy entrepreneur with a dream of dressing elegant women from head to toe.

He put his incredible creativity and exacting standards to use rekindling the French love of opulence and refinement, and building an empire in the process. By the time the designer passed away in 1957, the Dior brand encompassed not only clothes, but fragrances, shoes and hats.

Dior more than succeeded in his dream. In the decade he spent at the head of his own house, he revolutionised French fashion and took it to the world with breathtaking speed.

To return French couture to its glory days of luxury and excellence, Dior needed an intimate workshop.

The fledgling designer had a strong vision for the 'house' of Dior. It was to be small and secluded, with just a few workrooms where craftsmanship was the highest priority. And he knew just the place.

By chance, the business at 30 Avenue Montaigne, the building that Dior had walked past all those years ago, happened to be closing down in the very same week he was looking for a salon to call his own.

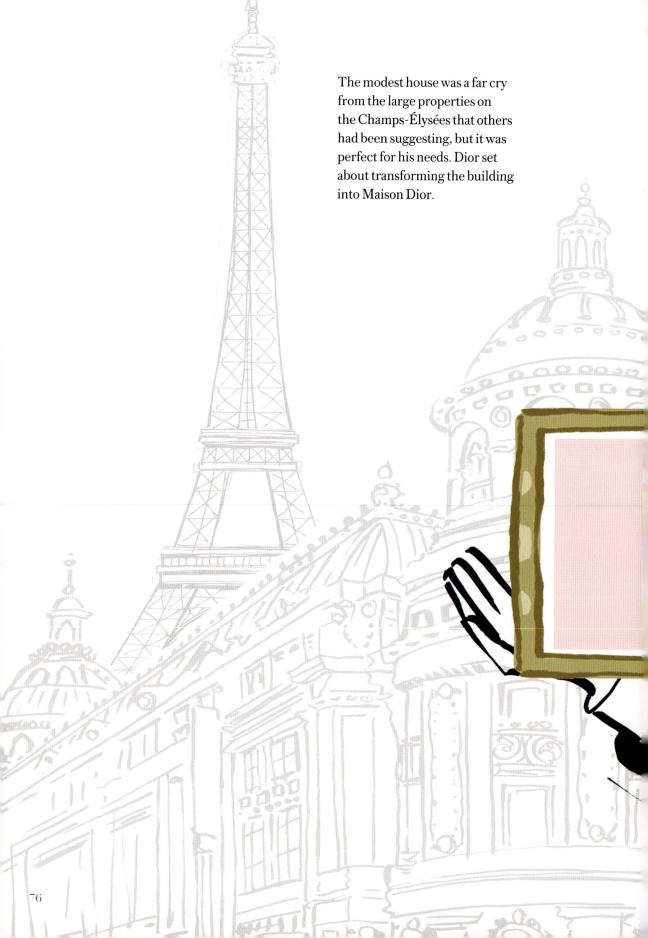

The modest house was a far cry from the large properties on the Champs-Élysées that others had been suggesting, but it was perfect for his needs. Dior set about transforming the building into Maison Dior.

His friend Victor Grandpierre
designed the interiors in
Neoclassical Louis XVI style,
which Dior had always loved.
And most importantly,
Dior hung his name
above the door.

Christian Dior

Dior began sketching and preparing for his opening show. He filled his ateliers with talented staff, and his total design vision and exacting standards quickly became legendary.

He often asked the *petites mains* and in-house models to work late into the night as they revived the labour-intensive traditions of couture.

Dior created masterpieces of craftsmanship as well as beauty.

Each detail was lovingly and painstakingly constructed, and no expense was spared.

Not satisfied with the shape of the seamstresses busts he had in the salon, he ordered new ones.

He smashed the busts
into shape with a hammer

and added extra padding to the hips in
order to achieve the curved dimensions
he wanted to exaggerate.

Everything had to be perfect for
the fashion revolution Dior was
about to launch.

"

By being natural AND SINCERE, one often can

create revolutions
WITHOUT HAVING
sought them.

"

On 12 February 1947, the first collection was ready.

Invitations to the show were highly coveted and crowds gathered at the salon to see what the new designer had to offer. The Avenue Montaigne headquarters were strewn with flowers for the event and every room smelled of Miss Dior – the fragrance that Dior had already started working on.

The audience took their places on rattan cannage chairs chosen specifically for the occasion.

It would be one of the most important debut collections ever shown, blowing away the utilitarian, rectilinear designs of the day and placing Maison Dior at the forefront of the glamorous years of fashion that were to come.

Over ninety styles were shown, split into two lines. Corolle was inspired by flowers, and En Huit, or 'figure eight', was inspired by a feminine silhouette and Dior's lucky number.

Dior

The silhouettes of the
collection were defined
by cinched waists, full
skirts, rounded shoulders
and accentuated busts.

The gowns were opulent and refined,
and the suits were structured and
impeccably tailored.

It was a radical departure from the plain,
unadorned fashions that had remained since
the difficult period of war and Depression.

The audience adored it.

Dior

Dior's friend Carmel Snow exclaimed:
'It's quite a revolution, dear Christian!
Your dresses have such a new look!'
A journalist overheard the quote and it
was published in the press the next day.

The revolutionary 'New Look' had its name.

The central pillar to the New Look collection
was the Bar Suit, an architectural marvel
named after the bar at the Plaza Athénée
that Dior liked to frequent.

The suit comprised a structured jacket
that emphasised the waist and hips, and a
full corolla skirt that used thirteen yards of
material (plus three yards of lining) folded
into accordion pleats, covering layers of tutu
tulle. Its creation required 150 hours of work.

"

The suit is
WITHOUT DOUBT
the most important
PIECE IN THE
female wardrobe.

"

Dior's debut might have been adored by the fashion industry, but it also caused a huge stir.

Journalists constantly asked Dior to justify his long hemlines, and feminists protested against the return to restrictive silhouettes after the freeing androgyny of the 1920s.

Others decried the abundant use of fabrics and embellishments.

However, with the controversy also came overnight success. Dior was suddenly in demand around the globe.

When Maison Dior opened, there were eighty-five people employed in the ateliers at 30 Avenue Montaigne. Seven years later, the company had expanded to occupy five floors, had twenty-eight workshops and employed over a thousand people.

It was a breathtaking rise.

Dior started work on his first
fragrance at the same time as
his debut collection.

Conceived as the very soul of his dresses, Miss Dior was present in the air when the debut collection launched.

At the perfume launch just months later, Dior staff sprayed an entire litre of the fragrance around the couture salons.

From that point on it was the signature scent of the house and today can be detected in any Dior boutique across the globe.

Miss Dior
Christian Dior

Christian Dior

Named in honour of Dior's brave younger sister Catherine, Miss Dior includes notes of gardenia, bergamot and jasmine: flowers reminiscent of the gardens where Christian loved to spend time with his mother at his childhood home in Granville.

In Dior's own words, it is a fragrance 'borne of those Provencal evenings alive with fireflies, where jasmine plays a descant to the melody of the night and land'.

The original curved Baccarat
bottle was designed to match
the feminine Dior silhouette.

It would later be replaced by
the geometric bottle when Dior
launched his vertical line in 1950.

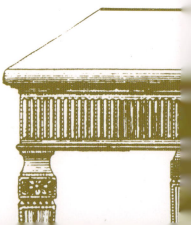

" A woman's perfume TELLS MORE about her than her HANDWRITING. "

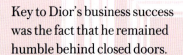

Key to Dior's business success
was the fact that he remained
humble behind closed doors.

As had been the case back
when he owned his galleries,
friendships were very important
to him, including the friendships
of his loyal staff.

Most important among
these were four women Dior
considered vital to his operations:

Madame Raymonde, director of
the designers' studio; Madame
Marguerite, his technical
director; Madame Bricard,
his muse and head of the hat
department; and his childhood
friend Suzanne Luling, who
oversaw the salons.

Dior was legendary for the kindness he displayed toward his employees and models, who he treated with fatherly care.

Some say he would step aside with a small bow to allow even the new apprentices to enter the elevator before him.

He made sure that his showrooms and ateliers at Avenue Montaigne were places his staff could feel at ease – even including a relaxation room for the models next to the studio.

The basement held a cafeteria where each employee paid according to what they earned, so that the food was affordable to all.

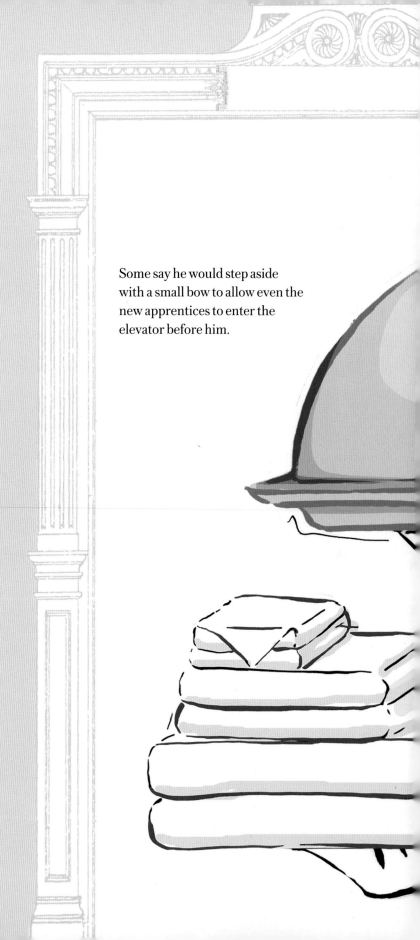

Dior commercialised French couture in a way none had dared try before, allowing his designs to be reproduced and sold in large quantities all around the world.

As an entrepreneur and ambassador for French fashion, he was often travelling.

The prophecy of that first clairvoyant that Dior visited way back in his teenaged years was finally coming true.

In 1948 he travelled to open
Christian Dior–New York,
which sold designs to suit clients
on that side of the Atlantic.

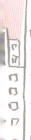

German-American actress Marlene Dietrich, Dior's friend and later neighbour at Avenue Montaigne, had attended his first fashion show in 1947.

At the time, *Elle* magazine ran a picture of her legs with a caption: 'We'll never see her gorgeous gams again because she ordered Dior's dresses and the longer hemline will cover them up!'

Dietrich remained faithful to Dior's designs both on stage and in her personal life. In 1950, Dior created every look for her in the Alfred Hitchcock film *Stage Fright*.

Grace Kelly

Dior had arrived in Hollywood and has
been a favourite of the silver screen ever since.
Grace Kelly wore a white satin Dior bustier
dress for her engagement in 1956.

Dior's popularity also quickly grew in London. It accelerated to fever pitch in the spring of 1950 when the house debuted its first British collection using all British fabrics.

Four thousand people applied for tickets to see the show at the Savoy Hotel.

Dior even gave a private viewing to the Queen and her younger sister. Princess Margaret became a loyal fan of the brand, famously wearing a Dior gown for her twenty-first birthday portrait.

BLENHEIM PALACE

In 1954 Dior put on a show at Blenheim Palace, and the next year he opened Christian Dior–London, cementing his affection for the country across the Channel. Dior said, 'I love English traditions, English politeness, English architecture. I even love English cooking.'

Dior's life became filled with travel and celebrations. In 1951, he attended the most famous party of the twentieth century with his old friend Salvador Dali.

The Beistegui Ball was a lavish costume party held by art collector Carlos de Beistegui in Venice.

Dior and Dali dressed each other for the occasion with the help of a then little-known designer called Pierre Cardin.

While Dior the man now exuded confidence, charm and ambition, the dreamy boy from Granville was never far below the surface.

Dior would retreat to the country before starting each new collection to create his designs in isolation. He claimed to sketch everywhere: 'in bed, in the bath, at the table, in the car, on foot, in the sun, under a lamp, during the day, at night'.

He often generated several hundred sketches before returning to Avenue Montaigne to begin the work of constructing the collection with the help of his dedicated team.

With every collection, Dior radically changed silhouettes – playing with hemlines, cinching, pleats and cuts to create fresh new lines every six months.

Each collection was named after its dominant line.

The Zig-Zag line featured slanted, diagonal cuts and pleats, the Envol ('flight') line included collars that evoked wings for taking off in flight, and the H line was straight up and down with only a slight accent on the waist.

"

It is one of the GREAT SECRETS of haute couture THAT A

well-cut dress
IS THE DRESS
which contains
THE LEAST CUTS.

"

Dior conceived of the structure of his dresses
like an architect and chose the colours like
a painter – unsurprising given his original
creative interests and experiences.

The twenty-two collections he produced
endlessly referenced his superstitions
and his childhood, particularly the house
at Granville, with flowers remaining a
special source of inspiration.

Dior loved lily of the valley so much that his regular florist would grow it in a greenhouse all year round just for him.

He would often be seen with a lily in his buttonhole, and he put dried sprigs of it in the hem of his haute couture skirts as a good-luck charm.

Dior also took to carrying a small cluster of talismans with him at all times – a four-leaf clover, a pair of hearts, a piece of wood and a gold star.

The original guiding star, the metal trinket he had hit his foot on the day he decided to open his own couture house, hung proudly in his workroom for all to see, and replicas would be given to long-serving staff.

It was a constant reminder of the role fate played in his life.

THE
LEGEND

CHRISTIAN DIOR PASSED AWAY unexpectedly in 1957, aged just 52. Although this tragically premature death meant that he spent only a decade at the helm of his own house, Dior had constructed a legend that would long outlive him.

Dior entrusted his young protégé, Yves Saint Laurent, to take over the collections. Saint Laurent and the five other designers who have led Dior since 1957 have been able to mine a rich vocabulary left to them by their founder: the structured silhouettes and elegant femininity that were at the core of everything Christian Dior created, and many other recurring motifs that have endured in the decades since he passed.

In remaining loyal to the brand's heritage and constantly revisiting Dior's early influences, each artistic director has ensured the legacy of Christian Dior remains as strong today as it ever was.

The fortune teller who had guided Dior in so many of his key decisions gave her famous patron one last prediction in 1957.

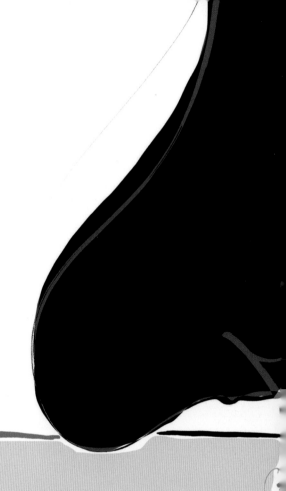

The couturier was planning to travel to Tuscany and she urged him not to go.

It was there that Dior passed away in October that year.

The fashion world immediately went into mourning.

Thousands of people attended Dior's funeral, and so many flowers were sent that the House of Dior was granted permission to lay them out under the Arc de Triomphe for all of Paris to see.

Dior left all his possessions to two women who had had such a big impact on his life: his sister Catherine and his right-hand woman, Madame Raymonde.

In line with the couturier's stated wishes,
21-year-old Yves Saint Laurent, who had been
working alongside his master for just two
years, took over as artistic director of Dior.

Despite the premature death of his mentor,
Saint Laurent had a strong framework upon
which to carry the house forward. For his
debut collection, Saint Laurent simplified
Dior's approach to couture and brought a
youthful freshness into it.

His creations had the same
perfect proportions and excellent
craftsmanship as Dior's, but they
were lighter, softer and easier
to wear.

He also shared Dior's predilection for
refashioning hemlines and silhouettes,
drastically changing cuts and lengths
with each new collection.

"

An ethereal
APPEARANCE
is only achieved by
ELABORATE
workmanship.

"

Marc Bohan took the reins in 1961 and was the longest-serving creative director at Dior, standing at the head for nearly three decades.

Bohan drove a lot of big developments in Dior, including introducing a menswear line.

His couture had an unmistakable refined elegance, characterised by the same luxurious use of fabrics as Dior himself.

Like Dior, Bohan also maintained
close links with Hollywood and
was a favourite of Elizabeth Taylor,
Sophia Loren and Grace Kelly.

Liz Taylor wore Dior to accept
the Oscar for best actress in 1961.

Elizabeth Taylor

DIOR

After Bohan came Gianfranco Ferré. Christian Dior would have been delighted to know that there was a trained architect at the helm of his brand. Ferré applied Dior's principles of structure and form.

His highly engineered pieces evoked the architectural designs of the New Look, and his version of Dior femininity was one of impeccable tailoring.

The ever-theatrical and controversial John Galliano was artistic director of Dior from 1996 to 2011. Galliano embraced Dior's revolutionary tendencies and always surprised his audiences with groundbreaking collections – just like the New Look had done in 1947.

Although he refused to abide by the status quo, Galliano also incorporated classic motifs in his designs, such as flowers – Dior's lifelong inspiration.

'I've often said that I am here to tend the blooms that he already planted,' Galliano told journalists backstage at his 2010 Autumn–Winter couture show, which was inspired by Dior's own Tulip line.

The next artistic director, Raf Simons,
also embraced the house's floral codes.
His debut show in 2012 was set against
a backdrop of a million flowers.

With a preference for minimalist design,
Simons embraced Dior's philosophy that
couture should be wearable.

Maria Grazia Chiuri became the very first woman to lead Dior when she took over in 2016, sixty-nine years after the brand's founding.

Chiuri has reinvigorated the label, but she has an unrivalled reverence for the house's founding father – Chiuri describes herself as 'fluent in the language of Dior'.

Her contemporary Bar Jackets and new iterations of classic bags and accessories have seen immense success for the brand.

"

INDIVIDUALITY
will always
BE ONE OF THE
conditions of
REAL ELEGANCE.

"

Dior's well-known superstitions have become house emblems and feature on everything from scarves and jewellery to entire couture collections.

Maria Grazia Chiuri is particularly fond of using these talismans as house codes. Her debut collection incorporated subtle references to Dior's superstitions and she has returned often to the influence that tarot cards had on the Dior story.

The cannage design, another enduring symbol of the house, has its genesis in the rattan chairs that Dior picked out for guests to sit on at his 1947 debut.

Later, he would experiment with the pattern for his own collections, eventually using it for the packaging for his perfume L'Eau Fraîche.

Dior's successors would come back to the cannage design through the decades, but its iconic status was cemented when Gianfranco Ferré used it as a topstitch on the Lady Dior handbag in 1994.

Today the design can be found on
everything from shoes and handbags
to lipsticks and eyeshadows.

The famous Lady Dior bag includes other nods to the house's famous father, such as the metallic charms attached to the strap, which evoke the good-luck talismans Dior used to carry on him at all times.

Bernadette Chirac, wife of French
President Jacques Chirac, commissioned
the bag as a gift for Princess Diana in 1995.

As the princess was regularly photographed
with this beautiful bag, it unsurprisingly
became a modern classic.

Dior designers have reinterpreted the Bar Jacket more than any other piece in the brand's history.

The iconic structure, with its cinched waist, basque bodice and sloping shoulders, is an eternal signature of Dior.

Yves Saint Laurent took a different approach with the Bar Jacket, elongating it and removing the waist in his Trapeze line. Other artistic directors have stayed true to the hourglass silhouette, but in a way that reflected their own style and that of the times.

Marc Bohan presented a soft pink version with cropped sleeves fit for the eighties. Gianfranco Ferré lengthened the jacket into a dress.

Galliano infused his versions with his usual theatrical approach, exploring maximalist textures and cuts, then Raf Simons pared it back for a minimalist take.

Maria Grazia Chiuri added a fluidity to the structure, ensuring her Bar Jackets are eminently wearable by today's women.

"

EVERYTHING
that has been
PART OF MY LIFE,
whether I wanted
IT TO OR NOT,
has expressed itself
IN MY DRESSES.

"

Despite constantly paying homage to designs of the 1940s
and 50s, the Dior of today is a brand that sits effortlessly in the
modern era. It is testament to the timelessness of elegance.

The original Miss Dior, Christian's much-loved younger sister Catherine, played a large role in his life, so it was only fitting that she too continued his legacy.

She moved to Château de La Colle Noire, a house Christian had bought near Grasse – the perfume capital of the world.

There she continued to farm the roses, jasmine and lavender for use in perfumes. She became well known as one of the only female cut-flower brokers in France and was a regular at Les Halles flower markets in Paris.

Catherine also became the honorary
president of the Musée Christian Dior.

Housed in the family's pink home in
Granville, it is the only museum in France
dedicated to a single couturier and shows a
permanent collection of Dior's best works.
The garden at Les Rhumbs is still filled
with lilies of the valley and roses, just as
Dior's mother intended.

Catherine continued as the honorary
president of the museum and a supporter of
Dior until she passed away aged ninety-one,
over fifty years after her brother's death.

Such was Catherine's importance to
the Dior story, Maria Grazia Chiuri
dedicated an entire collection to her
and her gardens in 2019.

Catherine
Dior

17. 06. 2008

Christian
Dior

24.10.1957

30 Avenue Montaigne remains at the heart of Dior and is a main source of inspiration for all its artistic directors.

Today people still travel from all over the world to visit the original House of Dior, in the city that Christian Dior loved, and to celebrate the incredible gift that Dior gave to the fashion world.

"

Happiness is THE SECRET to all beauty; THERE IS

no beauty that
IS ATTRACTIVE
without
HAPPINESS.

,,

Christia

ACKNOWLEDGEMENTS

To Emily Hart and Arwen Summers for creating another wonderful fashion book together. Thank you for making the process so much fun and for bringing so much enthusiasm to the project.

To Martina Granolic, thank you for diving head first into the world of Dior and for painstakingly piecing every single moment of his life together before we even started! For the hours, days and weeks spent creating this together, thank you.

To Andrea Davison for so beautifully researching, crafting and finding everything hidden about Dior's amazing life. Whenever I think I know a subject, you always show me that there's so much more. Thank you.

To Murray Batten, our eighth book together! Thank you once again for creating such a fresh and elegant design to house Dior's story. No-one makes text dance across a page like you!

To Todd Rechner for your incredible care and perfection in seeing my books to their finished form. You've made all of them something precious to hold, to read, to keep forever. Thank you.

To Justine Clay for first discovering my work and setting me on my way. I am forever grateful to have met you.

To my husband Craig and my children Gwyn and Will, thank you for listening to my endless talk of Dior, Bar Jackets, grey interiors, tarot cards and the magic a good luck charm can bring.

ABOUT THE AUTHOR

Megan Hess was destined to draw. An initial career in graphic design evolved into art direction for some of the world's leading advertising agencies and for Liberty London. In 2008, Megan illustrated Candace Bushnell's number-one-bestselling book *Sex and the City*. This catapulted Megan onto the world stage, and she began illustrating portraits for *The New York Times, Vogue Italia, Vanity Fair* and *TIME*, who described Megan's work as 'love at first sight'.

Today, Megan is one of the world's most sought-after fashion illustrators, with a client list that includes Givenchy, Tiffany & Co., Valentino, Louis Vuitton and *Harper's Bazaar*. Megan's iconic style has been used in global campaigns for Fendi, Prada, Cartier, Dior and Salvatore Ferragamo. She has illustrated live for fashion shows such as Fendi at Milan Fashion Week, Chopard at the 2019 Cannes Film Festival, Viktor&Rolf and Christian Dior Couture.

Megan has created a signature look for Bergdorf Goodman, New York, and a bespoke bag collection for Harrods of London. She has illustrated a series of portraits for Michelle Obama, as well as portraits for Gwyneth Paltrow, Cate Blanchett and Nicole Kidman. She is also the Global Artist in Residence for the prestigious Oetker Hotel Collection.

Megan illustrates all her work with a custom Montblanc pen that she affectionately calls 'Monty'.

Megan has written and illustrated eight bestselling fashion books, as well as her much-loved series for children, Claris the Chicest Mouse in Paris.

When she's not in her studio working, you'll find her dreaming of her next trip to 30 Avenue Montaigne in Paris to soak up a little more of the magic that Monsieur Dior first created.

———

Visit Megan at meganhess.com

Published in 2021 by Hardie Grant Books,
an imprint of Hardie Grant Publishing

Hardie Grant Books (Melbourne)
Building 1, 658 Church Street
Richmond, Victoria 3121

Hardie Grant Books (London)
5th & 6th Floors
52–54 Southwark Street
London SE1 1UN

hardiegrant.com/au/books

 A catalogue record for this
book is available from the
National Library of Australia

Christian Dior
ISBN 978 1 74379 726 6

10 9 8 7 6

Publisher: Arwen Summers
Project Editor: Emily Hart
Researcher: Andrea Davison
Designer: Murray Batten
Design Manager: Mietta Yans
Production Manager: Todd Rechner

Colour reproduction by Splitting Image Colour Studio
Printed in China by Leo Paper Products LTD.

 The paper this book is printed on is from FSC®-certified forests and
other sources. FSC® promotes environmentally responsible, socially
beneficial and economically viable management of the world's forests.

Hardie Grant acknowledges the Traditional Owners of the country on which we work,
the Wurundjeri people of the Kulin nation and the Gadigal people of the Eora nation,
and recognises their continuing connection to the land, waters and culture. We pay our
respects to their Elders past, present and emerging.